More Praise for
When a Purple Rose Blooms

"Jeneé Darden's *When a Purple Rose Blooms* is a daring book of poems and essays, depicting family, pop culture, self-love, racism, and other issues, especially those that impact women. This truth-telling book heralds with allusions, historical references, blues, East Oakland, and intergenerational camaraderie, praise, and 'God's Image.' These poems and essays tell us what's happening, and display much intelligence."

– LENARD D. MOORE, author of *The Geography of Jazz*, Associate Professor of English, University of Mount Olive

When a Purple Rose Blooms

Jeneé Darden

NOMADIC
PRESS

NOMADIC PRESS

OAKLAND

111 FAIRMOUNT AVENUE
OAKLAND, CA 94611

BROOKLYN

475 KENT AVENUE #302
BROOKLYN, NY 11249

WWW.NOMADICPRESS.ORG

MASTHEAD

FOUNDING AND MANAGING EDITOR
J. K. FOWLER

ASSOCIATE EDITOR
MICHAELA MULLIN

DESIGN
J. K. FOWLER

COMMUNITY EDITOR
MK CHAVEZ

MISSION STATEMENT

Nomadic Press is a 501 (C)(3) not-for-profit organization that supports the works of emerging and established writers and artists. Through publications (including translations) and performances, Nomadic Press aims to build community among artists and across disciplines.

SUBMISSIONS

Nomadic Press wholeheartedly accepts unsolicited book manuscripts. To submit your work, please visit www.nomadicpress.org/submissions

DISTRIBUTION

Orders by trade bookstores and wholesalers:
Small Press Distribution,
1341 Seventh Street
Berkeley, CA 94701
spd@spdbooks.org
(510) 524-1668 / (800) 869-7553

When a Purple Rose Blooms

This book was made possible by a loving community of chosen family and friends, old and new.

For author questions or to book a reading at your bookstore, university/school, or alternative establishment, please send an email to info@nomadicpress.org.

Cover and back artwork by Arthur Johnstone

Published by Nomadic Press, 111 Fairmount Avenue, Oakland, CA 94611

Third printing, 2019

Printed in the United States of America

LIBRARY OF CONGRESS CATALOGING-IN-PUBLICATION DATA

Darden, Jeneé 1979 –
Title: *When a Purple Rose Blooms*
P. CM.
Summary: *When a Purple Rose Blooms* is a collection of poetry and essays that reflect writer Jeneé Darden's journey through Black womanhood. Through heart and humor, Darden engages us in conversations about race, love, sex, and mental health. Like a rose, being a Black woman in this society comes with its thorns and beauty. Darden brings that complexity to every page.

[1. BLACK WOMANHOOD. 2. RACE. 3. LOVE. 4. MENTAL HEALTH. 5. AMERICAN GENERAL.] I. III. TITLE.

2018958529

ISBN: 978-1-7327866-0-8

When a Purple Rose Blooms

Jeneé Darden

NOMADIC
PRESS

*for the little Black girl in East
Oakland with the pink bedroom*

CONTENTS

MY LOVIN'

SELF-ESTEEM

Men been leaving her
Since she entered the world
Her daddy split right after the doctor said
It's a girl

Her 1st boyfriend left her for Alexis
Her 2nd boyfriend left her for Dallas, Texas
Her 3rd boyfriend left her for Travis

Her fiancé left her for the bottle and the nice girl on 85th
With a blonde weave

All she knew about men were they lie
They leave

And their hearts had a short attention span for her love

What's wrong with me?!
She cried to her friends
What's wrong with me?

Girl, they'd say
You just need some self-esteem

Huh? Self-esteem?
Where do you get that? she asked

Is it something you buy off the rack?
Do they sell it at Big Lots
Next to discounted Baby Phat?

Hmmm...self-esteem

Does it come in a lotion bottle?

Or a jar?
Like beauty cream
Has Oprah given it way in her Favorite Things?

Can I get it at the Slauson Swap Meet?
Or Durant Square?

Is it easy to put on?
Like a clip in my hair
Hold up!
Does it come with my Obama Care?

Do I eat it?
Do I wear it?
Do I hang it on the wall?
Is it available year around?
Winter, spring, summer, fall?

Is it free?
Do I have to pay?

Don't play!

Does it fall from the sky or grow from the ground?
Maybe mine is in some lost and found
Is it something I can hold?
Will it make me feel good?
Do they make it for rich girls
And us girls in the hood?

Is there a commercial for it?
A jingle? A song?
Can I order it from Amazon?

Get some self-esteem. You make it seem easy
She said to her friends

You make it sound like it's the answer
Without a doubt

But how is self-esteem the key in a world
That constantly tries
To lock Black women out?

Now this is where the poem ends
Because when looking for self-esteem
Where does one begin?

MY FEMININE SIDE

I.

Every morning, until I turned 18, I woke up in a sanctuary. A sanctuary in East Oakland made of carnation pink walls. Every morning the soft matching carpet brushed the bottoms of my feet. Every morning I gazed up at the Black art, Superman picture and TLC poster sharing space on my pink walls. I was a girly-girl nerd and multimedia diva in the making. My desk was a crystal ball with symbols of my future: a word processor, journals and Terry McMillan novels.
I was the only child in my family for a long time. Talk about overprotection. Even with bars on my window, I never felt more free than in my sanctuary—where I planted the seeds of my femininity.

II

I'm Granddaddy's baby
A Cali girl with Southern roots
I love Talk of the Town burritos and Grandma's mustard greens
I'm hella Oakland
I watched Grandma turn her laundry room into a hair salon
And sell Avon from her kitchen
I'm pressed edges and cherry lip gloss
I smell like Creme of Nature and honeysuckle
I love charm school and cussin'

I'm Honor Roll
So are my boobs
Straight A's
Get it?
God, I want bigger boobs
I'm an insecure, high-achiever
I'm mommy's girl
She protects me from men who make me feel uncomfortable
(But you have to watch out for bad women too)

I'm invisible
An only child
I'm overprotected
I sneak to meet boys
And I get caught
Sometimes

I secretly watch HBO's *Real Sex* in my sanctuary
Oooooh, Ohhhh
Part of me is ashamed
A very small part of me
I want more female empowerment like
Queen Latifah and Lauryn Hill
I see feminism in my history book
Not in my neighborhood
I'm for it
But I'm not sure if it's
For me

I'm a woman now
A grown-ass woman
Still prissy and nerdy

Some men see women as prey
I'm the prey that got away
Barely
Kind of
I wish I learned how to fight

I'm a woman now
I'm angry about a lot of shit
It makes me sad

I want more female empowerment
I seek it for years
Am I a Feminist?

I'm a woman
Don't put me on Team Mary or
The other Team Mary
I'm more complex than that
I think I may be a Womanist

I'm a woman
With pink walls and a gold heart
I want to be pleasured,
Loved
Respect me

BE

Be Divine
Bleed for days and never die
Because you are life
Bringing life
In all forms

Be the first path a human travels
From a black hole
In the galaxy that is your body

Be strong
Leather tight
Be soft and stretchy
Dry and juicy
Warm as the skin
Of your inner thighs
When they come together
Like hands in prayer

Be Eve's Daughter
Black plum with a dark cherry middle
Blessed with a pleasure center
That peaks between brown lips
A pearl holding 8,000 volts of satisfaction
Firing off from the perfect slight touch
You call God's name
Because you feel close to Heaven
Then baptize your lover
In your nectar

Be interested
Or not

Be still

Be protected
Under a jungle of
Wild brush
Or by a manicured bush
Or bare it all

Be unapologetic and self-assured
There are people
Who fear your greatness
Think they can exploit you
Want to control you

Be armed with knowledge of
Where you come from
Who you are

Be your own definition

Be connected to your body and spirit
Love getting loved on
With tongues and kisses
Turned on by fingers and phallus
Dominant or docile

The ones you invite
To enter your temple
Must bow in respect

Be Beautiful
Unashamedly Black and sweet

Be in awe of yourself
Be

BATTLEGROUND

After the smoke cleared
I stood in the battlefield
Littered with broken, thorny stems
And crushed purple rose petals
On a ground saturated in
Tears
The smell of burning books
And my favorite skirt
Stung my nostrils
Torn paintings stole my hope
Until I saw a bush of deep, purple roses across the way
And *Barefoot Dreams[1]* held between the leaves
I walked toward the bush
Past the fallen soldiers I overpowered
I walked on the ground stained with their blood
My royal red carpet
Their amputated hands can't touch me anymore
I went to the rosebush
Kneeled down in the soil
Beholding my *Barefoot Dreams*
I saw the girl
Her white bows and plaited hair
Finally
Visions of my womanhood are coming true
My I've come a long way
From when...

They said Black girls from East Oakland are supposed to be tough.
Daintiness is not an option. Feeling pain is not an option. They said my
sensitivity was *on some white girl shit* and Black women don't have time
to be depressed. Bright colors and pastels aren't an option on dark skin.
Beauty is not an option for dark girls.
Stay your crow-colored ass out of the sun!
But my darkness absorbs all that is light and warm. The sun loves shining

on me.

I fought the world to embrace myself. I purged the poisonous messages in my brain that said my love for dresses, makeup and pretty things was wrong for girls like me. I purged poisonous messages that said women who look like me are never loved. Thank God Truth set me free.
Sojourner Truth asked, *Ain't I a woman? Sista, ain't you a woman?*
I thought about it.
Well, hell yeah!
I gave myself permission to be *my* definition of woman. What an act of love. Truth cured me. Truth set me free.

I fought the world to embrace those warm feelings from my center. The ones that feel like flying comets traveling throughout every part of your body, and bursting into a blazing orange light.

Sexual feelings weren't an option for a Catholic schoolgirl, from a Baptist family. Liking boys wasn't an option.
Baby girl, stick to the books and the Bible. Stay out of your flesh.

Thank God writers put naughty stuff in books. Thank God Black women write erotica and romance. I had to purge the poison again. Lorde delivered me. Audre Lorde said women have power in the erotic. I gave myself permission to bring passion and pleasure to all areas of my life. I connected spirit to my body. Lorde delivered me. Lorde delivered me from shameful feelings.

God never stopped loving me.

1. *Barefoot Dreams* is a painting by Brenda Joysmith

PINK CONFESSIONS
for all those girls who were told they were too dark

I must confess and apologize for the little white lie I believed
Because holding something inside that should come to light
Only gives me the blues

That secret I've been keeping for so long
Is not dark
But pink

Yes, me
Cocoa, Dark Brown, Sexy Chocolate me
LOVES PINK
The color pink

*I now present to you my pink confession*s

I'm almost ashamed to admit this
But I've been tricked into thinking that the color pink was only restricted
To the Honey Comb, Light Brown, or Sunny Blonde shades that were
not me

It looked good on Barbie
And the light skinned girl
Who sat in the front of my class
But when I *dared* to wear my favorite color to class
(Or any bright color for that matter)
I only got teases and laughs

They said I was trying to be an African
And pink was too *feminine* for a dark-skinned girl like me

But hold up!
Aren't my ancestors African?
Ain't I girly, girly?
Why can't the two co-exist?

You mean it's okay for me to admire it
But never let it rest on my skin?

I refused to let pink be admired
Without it being admired on me

You see
Me and pink
We have a history
It's the color you see under a healing scab
The sky's hue at sunset
The tint of orchid and rose
It's the spotting I first saw at 13
The deep shade that sparkles
Between my thighs

It's the first lipstick some girls wear
As a child, it was my favorite pair of underwear
It's the carpet that cushions between my toes
And the only beads I let my Momma put in my hair

In my world pink is everywhere

Ohh, but when I rock it
You better beware
Because the power, sophistication, and sexiness
That radiates from me
Gets people's attention

My pink, cocoa brown, rapture
Got men breaking their necks
To look in my direction!

Years later this dark sister proclaims

I'm gonna wear my pink anyway!
Honestly, I slay in a hue of rose
Any day

I don't care what they said

Fuchsia, Rose, Carnation,
Empowering, Soft, Beauty,
Serenity
All Make Up Me

I will never deprive myself of shine and color
Because of what they think
Because the truth is
I can rock the hell
Out of some pink

BETWEEN HERE AND SILENT PRAYERS

Lying on the table
My feet tremble in stirrups
Stark white table paper
Crackles under my back

The doctor chatters
Fast
Like a con artist

To her I am not a patient
But an experiment
A paragraph she highlighted
In her med-school book

I'm a slab of meat
She slices me inside
With dull blades
Like a rookie butcher
My cervix is the part of the animal
Nobody wants

She ignores my cries to stop
I am a body
A living cadaver to her
A diagram she memorized in med school
Just darker
Like the faceless women who flood my mind
My spirit
Dr. Sims' victims from centuries ago

This doctor knows
Nothing about
That part of history

She could care less

I leave my body
Floating between here
And silent prayers

The snapping sounds of her
Bloody latex gloves
Bring me back

All done, she says
I'm crossed off her task list

Red drops roll from
Between my legs
My body is crying
She tosses the gloves onto the bloody blades and exam table
So many red tears

She gives a fake smile of accomplishment
Hands me wipes
As she leaves
I am sore
Body shaking
Mind confused

Stunned
I dress
And *get out*
Holding my stomach
I limp to the nurse's station
She is annoyed by
My request for Tylenol
I am just a body to her too

Am I the only one?
I can't be
I am not

The doctor carved my flesh
Not my voice
And that's sharper
Than any blade

I may be weary
But I'm not afraid to use it.

WARRIORS IN DRESSES

Don't get it twisted
And mistake these
Glossy lips and dainty walk
For weakness
I come from warriors
In dresses
Full faced in Fashion Fair
Suited in their Sunday best
Booted in heels
And pantyhose
Wearing church hat helmets
On top of press and curled hair
Toting clutch bags for shields
Covered in the armor of God
Singing Battleground Hymns from the church and mosque
Leading the fight for freedom
They stood on the front lines for justice

Generals Evers, Shabazz and King
General Hamer
General Height
General Daisy Bates
Special Agent Baker

World changers and not a hair out of place

Their legacy is still recruiting

Enlist

LOVE AT FIRST BREATH

I left the womb
Riding on a wave of blessings
Welcomed into this world
By God, my mother and grandmother

With my mother I felt love at first heartbeat
For my grandmother
It was love at first breath

This poem is for her
My grandmother
A Mississippi girl with California dreams
She picked cotton on her family farm
As planes flew overhead she'd say
One day I'm going to get on one of them planes and get outta here
She followed her courageous heart out West
To the warmth of other suns

This poem is for the woman known as Angie, Auntie, Mama, Sista
Bama
The nickname I gave her
When my baby tongue couldn't pronounce
Grandma

This poem is for my Bama
A Country Gal who always kept a pan of cornbread in the oven
A Southern Belle living in a home designed for a queen
She never let her purse out of her sight
A Stylish lady with berry tinted lips, pearl earrings
And fingernails that glistened like rubies on her chocolate brown skin

This poem is for my grandmother
An entrepreneur who turned her laundry room into a hair salon
Her den into a daycare

And delivered Avon from her car
She pressed our hair
Greased our scalps with Ultra Sheen
Honey, my grandmother carried Black Girl Magic
Before it had a name

This poem is for my grandmother
On morning rides to school in her silver Thunderbird
We praised the Lord with Mighty Clouds of Joy
B.B. King and Aretha took us home in the afternoons

Where she loved watching her soaps
A bold and beautiful woman
My grandmother loved all of her children

This poem is for my Bama
Made of brown sugar and a whole lot of spice

Dementia may have stopped her from remembering the day of the week
But my grandmother never forgot she had it going on
On occasion she'd say to me
I can still get a boyfriend

Lord, bless me with that level of confidence

My dearest Bama, this poem is for you
No ashes to ashes or dust to dust
When God saw you
He said
Angie to Angel

Angie to Angel
My love at first breath

YOU CAN'T STOP ME FROM SOARING

In the beginning
I was a small flower pot
Filled with rich soil
Fertile with possibility

You nurtured me
You, my gardeners of life
Dropped seeds of knowledge and women's empowerment
Seeds of courage and self-love
Seeds of Spirit

Strong seeds in a sexist, racist world
That couldn't stop this Black girl

Over time my petals bloomed
Larger than palm leaves
Then into wings
Can you believe it?
WINGS
My flower pot couldn't hold me
I was ready to fly
Shine

Just as I was about to take flight
Life slammed me down
I reached out my hand
Praying you were around
Instead you were behind me
Turning the blades in my back
My soul bled every second
But I can't go back
In time
To what I thought you were
We were

All lies
I mourned my past life
As you kept turning
The knife

You rained down on me your fears and envy
You called my wisdom
Foolish
My confidence
Weak
My Blackness
Oversensitive
You called my womanhood
Whorish

How dare I try for the sky
When you really wanted me down
Deep in your barrel of regret for bad choices made
And unfulfilled dreams.

But as Maya Angelou said
My description cannot fit your tongue
For I have a certain way of being in this world

See, you forgot you're dealing with
An unstoppable girl
A woman on fire
A Phoenix
No my name ain't Jean Grey
But me
Jeneé
I'm just as powerful
I can't be contained

Your life's sores
Won't stop me from soaring
From Praying
From Healing

Your life's sores won't stop me from soaring

Ever.

Move out of the way

There's my sky

FOR NIA WILSON AND OUR FALLEN ROSES

I GREW UP IN THE '90S watching shows like *Def Comedy Jam* and BET's *Comic View*. Good relationship jokes got lots of laughs. A common joke about Black women was the consequences of hitting a sista during an argument. The comedians said Black women have no tolerance for abuse. We raise our fists and don't hold our tongues. Slap a Black woman's face and our head revolves around like a scene from *The Exorcist*. I remember one comedian compared the outcome of hitting a Black woman, to getting in a fight with Bruce Lee. Somehow Black women possessed special martial arts powers that could take down anyone, including a man.

This stereotype of Black women didn't start with Black comedy shows. The strong, angry, masculine labels put on Black women date back to slavery. However, the danger of these stereotypes is they erase the truth. Malcolm X said the most disrespected, unprotected and neglected person in America is the Black woman. Why protect, respect and care for a person that is stereotyped as someone who neither needs, nor deserves, such treatment? The truth is we do need and deserve all of this.

Black women are made of steel, yet a Washington University study found nearly 60 percent of black women killed by law enforcement from 2013–2015 were unarmed.

If Black women are such bad bitches, why are we subject to higher rates of psychological abuse, sexual assaults and intimate partner violence compared to women of other races?[1]

If ALL Black women can hold their own, why was 18-year-old Nia Wilson stabbed to death at Oakland's MacArthur BART Station on the way home from a family party? Why did the violent man choose to attack

Nia and her sister Letifah Wilson if we are to be feared? Why is Letifah left with deep scars?

Why are so many of us afraid?

1. Green, Susan. "Violence Against Black Women—Many Types, Far- Reaching Effects." Institute for Women's Policy Research. 13 July 2017. https://iwp.org

MY STRENGTH

My strength is not a choice
Or your over exaggerated expectations
Of some fable you read
I am not made of vibranium
Who told you dark skin doesn't bruise?
Or Black bones don't shatter?

My strength is not a choice
My sass is not here for your amusement
Or your imitation
It's fun playing Black girl
Learning my slang from Twitter
Your costume doesn't come with invisible bullseyes
Over your forehead
Between your legs
On your back
Those are the few I know of
Where are you when the blood sheds?
Riding the outbound train
You're never around when the blood sheds

My strength is not a choice
I'm neither here to serve you
Nor save you
I don't carry your problems
And the weight of the world
In a small clutch for Saturday night

Don't believe the myth
I am not here to make sacrifices
Feeding me scraps from a trough
So you can eat from silver platters
Then gorge on my soul
Does not serve humankind

Find another mule

My strength is not a choice
But a life strategy passed down
Sometimes a shield
Or an invisible cloak
Wrapped around my suffering
Although it's you that
Erase me

Somebody see ME
So one day they won't to have to
Say my name

DAYS AFTER SHE WAS stabbed and her sister murdered, survivor Letifah Wilson spoke at a press conference.

She said, "*As young Black women we shouldn't have to look behind our backs 24/7. We should be living free like everybody else. Why everybody else get to live freely?*"

I would add, why has joy and self-care become an act of resistance? Think about it. We live in a society where some people are so contemptuous of Black folks for living joyfully, they the call the police on us for doing everyday things. Black people grocery shopping, eating in restaurants, mowing lawns to make money, laughing on a wine train in Napa, reading a book, walking home and praising God in church are a few examples. The list keeps getting longer.

Audre Lorde said, "*Caring for myself is not self-indulgence, it is self-preservation, and that is an act of political warfare.*"

We live in a country where Black people enjoying life is a crime to some, and an act of resistance for others.

JOY

When times get tough
I go hard on getting joy
Call the girls to go out
Play Janelle Monae

Electric ladies
Cruise to rooftop parties
Drink Bacardi
Sip on some Goose

At the family beach barbecue
Kissing the new babies
Dancing to '90s hip hop
In flip flops

Cupid Shuffle
Electric Slide
See my cousin pull up
In his new ride

Give him the Wakanda salute
Check out the friend he brought
He's really cute

Touch up my Fenty gloss
Sashay in my African skirt
Flash a bright smile
I'm ready to flirt

Blue skies, golden sands
Sun rays glowin' on my skin
Thanking God for the melanin

Nappy hair
I care
For it
Lovin' me in braids, weave,
An Afro

Gotta carry the self love
Everywhere I go

Essence Fest to Paris
Comic Con to Johannesburg
Saturday nights on the Vegas Strip to
Sunday mornings learning the Word

After service visit Grandma Jean
For girl talk and her
Spicy collard greens

She slices soft, warm cornbread
With a crispy bottom crust
Loved baked in an
Iron cast skillet
I don't take these moments
For granted

Living with attitude and gratitude
I'm Queenin'
Only caring about what I think
I'm Queenin'
Living my best life despite the strife
I'm Queenin'
Accepting I stand out in the crowd

While keeping my Mama proud
I'm Queenin'
Not gonna let this world keep me down
I'm Queenin'
I'm Queenin'
I'm Queenin'

I SAW NIA WILSON'S Facebook page. She was Queenin' with her hairstyles and makeup skills. Nia's family gave her a royal goodbye. Her last ride in Oakland was in a coffin, on a horse-drawn carriage.

It doesn't matter if you're from the projects or the suburbs. Doesn't matter if you drive a Benz or ride BART.

James Baldwin said, "*Our crown has already been bought and paid for. All we have to do is wear it.*"

We wear our crowns.

When society tells Black women that we don't fit the image of what a queen, a woman or anyone worthy of respect should be—I remind myself that we're made in God's image.

IN GOD'S IMAGE
inspired by the "Black Woman is God" exhibit

I entered the temple
My spirit and heart first
And joined others like me
Searching for God

We searched for God
Her skin color of midnight, Earth and sunrays
We searched for God
Her hair long, locked, twisted
Like rainforest vines
Short and gloriously poofy
Bald and smooth
Flowing like the rivers and waterfalls
She created

We searched for God
Breast, thighs
Thick lips
Booty
Broad nose
Stretch marks
Cellulite
Womb and wombless
Full of life
Her body had no boundaries
No flaws

She divinely carried rhythm
Unique only to Her

We searched for God's heart
That spans galaxies and galaxies
Granting us to love who we desire

We heard God pray for us
She sounds like Oakland, the 9th Ward
Brixton and Brooklyn
Ladera Heights and South Central
Cuba and Ghana

We ask God for strength
We ask God
Who are you?

She whispers
I Am

I Am

Then she whispers our names
Our sisters' names
I am Sandra and Mitrice
I am Latasha and Tamika
I am Imani and Sofia

I Am

I fall to my knees breathless
Tears streaming
I look around
I am surrounded by my reflection
My God
My God
My God

MENTAL PICTURE
to my anxiety

I wish my mind
Looked something
Different

Like
Blue birds gliding over wide southern fields
Or a child walking barefoot in her Granny's yard

Maybe I want my mind to look like a string of pearls
Hanging loosely off a Renaissance lady
About to hit the Harlem streets
Shimmering and flowy

I wish my mind
Mirrored the first feel of silk on a tired hand
Or a pretty scarf tied around a woman's crown
So soft

I want the spirals of my mind to look less like the twists of a storm
And more like God's design on a snail's shell
Whimsical

My mind
I wish
Looked like the red hues on autumn's leaves
Or plushy slippers on Mama's feet after a long workday

The first sip of warm tea
A kind stranger's smile
A baby's first giggle

I wish my mind
Looked something
Different

GROWING UP DARDEN

"*ARE YOU GOING TO watch this O. J. show?*" I asked my father over drinks.

"*Nope.*"

"*Why?*" I asked, though I should have known what he would answer.

"*I lived it.*"

I was 15 years old in 1994 when my father, Christopher Darden, joined the prosecution team against O.J. Simpson, a case very much in the news again thanks to "The People vs. O.J. Simpson," now airing on FX. To say the least, it was a turbulent time for me: the daughter of a black prosecutor, prosecuting a successful black man in the trial of the 20th century.

I grew up in East Oakland, in a mostly black and Latino neighborhood. My parents never married and I lived with my mother. Life before the trial was simple. Our street had less crime compared to other blocks in the area, and all I wanted in life were straight A's, a boyfriend who shared my love for X-Men cartoons, and TLC concert tickets. As the racial tensions surrounding the case grew, so did my anxiety. I worried the students at my predominantly black high school would harass me when they found out about my father. Many black people sided with Simpson and thought my father was a traitor.

Most of my classmates told me, "I don't agree with what your daddy is doing, but you're cool so I support you." But not everyone felt compassion. While walking down the stairs after class one day, a black kid stopped me on the steps when other students were around. He said to my face, "Dude, I'm sorry, but your father is a Tom. A straight up sellout." Then he strutted away as if he'd accomplished something. Embarrassment and shock left me speechless.

On the flip side, black people who suspected I was related to "that Darden" and believed Simpson was guilty would whisper conspiratorially in my ear. "I think he did it," they'd say, "but don't tell anyone I told you that." They feared others would consider them sellouts, too.

I understood why many black people, especially black people in Los Angeles, supported Simpson. I remember the beating of Rodney King and the shooting death of Latasha Harlins, 15, over a bottle of orange juice. Like today, black folks were tired of racially motivated killings. Still it hurt to see my father, a proud black man who encouraged me to embrace my heritage, be called a traitor. My father wanted justice for victims Nicole Brown and Ron Goldman.

I admired my father's courage in the chaos. He received death threats but never let on that he was concerned.

"*Are you O.K.?*" I asked my father over the phone.

"*Don't worry about me. I just want to make sure you're safe,*" he calmly replied so I wouldn't panic. It didn't work.

My parents told my school about the threats and asked security officers to keep their eyes open. We postponed visits to Los Angeles. The O. J. trial became more than a trial, it became a national spectacle, and I desperately hoped it would end quickly. It lasted more than eight months.

When my family wasn't praying through death threats, we were dealing with the media. Strange-looking men rang my mother's doorbell for the scoop on my dad. Paparazzi called my private line, an unlisted number—I have no idea how they found it.

"*Hi, is this Jenee?*" a woman asked in the condescending tone adults use with toddlers.

"*Who is this?*"

"*We're from a magazine. You want to tell us some stuff about your daddy?*"

I hung up.

My mother loved reading gossip pages in the grocery store. I found them silly. But guess who landed in a tabloid? "*FOUND! Doting Dad Darden's Secret Love Child*" covered the front page of one rag. Apparently, they found my conception out of wedlock newsworthy. I was never a secret. I opened the magazine to see a page-length photo of me in my winter ball gown. A black bar covered my eyes because I was a minor. Next to me was a picture of my uncle's ex-wife, who'd sold the photo to the tabloid.

A few days later, I headed to my locker before the homeroom bell. I passed a cluster of students huddled around copies of the tabloid, reading the "article" about me. They tried to hide it before I saw them. They thought it was cool. I found it bizarre and uncomfortable.

But my experience is nothing compared to what my father's other relatives endured. Paparazzi hounded my uncle while he suffered with

AIDS. They even had the audacity to call my grandparents and ask how they felt about my uncle's illness while he was on his deathbed. He passed away the month after the trial ended.

The public's emotions remained raw long after the trial. Since I didn't know if people I came across hated my father, I rarely told anyone I was his daughter.

"*Hey, I noticed your last name is Darden,*" said the short, middle-aged black man from my Bay Area fitness class in 2003. I knew what was coming next.

"*Are you related to Chris Darden, the bald-headed guy from the O. J. trial?*"

I gave my usual response.

"*Oh, no,*" I lied.

"*Good,*" he said while pounding his clenched fist into his palm. "*Man, if I ever saw that [racial slur], I'd ...*"

Unlike my father, I'm watching the FX miniseries. I'm too curious to refrain. On the whole I find it captivating, but my concern is the same as ever—that the drama surrounding the case overshadows the brutal deaths of two people. Whether you think Simpson is guilty or innocent, Ron Goldman's family lost a son and brother. Nicole Brown's children are without a mother. There's nothing glamorous about that at all.

MY THREE WISE MEN
for my grandfathers

The three wise men
I know and love
Grew up on Texas farms
Snacked on caviar
They fished out of the
Mississippi Gulf

They had Golden State dreams
Rushed out West
Hoping to hit the jackpot
Opportunity

They folded up their
Smarts
Charm
Barbecue recipes
And carried them
In their back pockets

Somewhere along their journey
I came along
Blessed to be a student
Of these three wise men
A princess from three kings

THE GIFT

One Sunday afternoon
While happily lost
In a pile of Transformers, dolls and
My 7-year-old imagination
My mother came to me
With something in her hand
Bubelah, I have a present for you

It didn't light up, but it made me shine
It couldn't hear, but it listened to me
It couldn't talk, but it gave me a voice
It was nothing fancy, but it came from a beautiful place
It cost her nothing, but I knew it was precious
It wasn't made of crystal, but it reflected me
It didn't come with batteries, but it empowered me

She gave me a six-ring binder
Small and brown like me
She filled it with pages
Typed up a label at work with my name
Taped it perfectly front and center
A book with my name on the cover
My first journal
She told me
Write down your feelings
Write about anything you want

My mother planted something
In me
Years ago
It still blossoms

THE MOURNING AFTER 11/9

The young wailing woman
Rushes outside
Barefoot
Cracking the morning's quiet
Awakening those
Hung over with headaches and blurred rosy vision
From the post-racial punch
They guzzled over the years

The woman wails
Screams in rage
Because she tried to tell them
But they didn't listen to her
They never listen to women who look like her
Even though she comes from people
Who walked Earth the longest

The woman wails
Barefoot on the shoulders
Of her mother, grandmother, great-grandmother
Generations and generations apart
Yet she cries the same tears
As the women before her

Her cries of rage
Reach the ears of women she can't see
They understand and envy her
These women are suffocating on screams locked in their throats
Wishing they could shatter the skies with their own cries

She yells
Throws up her arms
Summoning praying women
Of the temple, church, mosque, shrines

Praying women of the earth

They encircle her with bare feet and strong hearts
The young woman weeps on holy ground
They are doing what comes naturally
Swaying and humming
Barefoot
Like their grandmothers and great-grandmothers did
On plantations
In prisons and missions
At the graves
All where trees bear strange fruit

The young woman cries
The praying women sway
Humming spirituals

Like their great-grandmothers, grandmothers and mothers
They wonder
When will God deliver us?

BLACK WINGS AND WHITE LIES
for my great, great granfather

Grandma told me
Strange fruit grows on our family tree
Your secrets buried
In my DNA

I always felt something
Things make more sense now
Yet leave me with more questions

The wise woman with the
Crown of grey locs told me
My body is a book
I should find the answers inside

I inherited your pain and perseverance
Depression and anxiety
Do we share a spirit of self-pride?

I've carried you for so long
Now I see it's you
Who stirs my spirit every time I step
On that Fruitvale BART platform

It's you who stirred in my spirit
When the white woman called the cops
On the Black men barbecuing

When I read
The white woman confessed
She lied about Emmett Till
It was you
Whispering to me
That's my story, too

White lies clip black wings
Because they fear
We can fly higher than them

I carry your doubts that change for the better is coming
I share your hope for a future
Where these pains stay in the past

I'M DEPRESSED BECAUSE I DON'T HAVE A GOOD RELATIONSHIP WITH GOD?

GROWING UP IN THE church, I heard ministers say, "*Don't take your problems to a psychologist. Take them to Jesus.*" Or, "*If you're feeling depressed you just need to pray harder.*" There was this notion that somehow your mental health problems were a result of you not being prayed up enough or having a weak connection to God. They also assumed depression was a choice. But I never heard preachers say to church members diagnosed with cancer, "*Don't get radiation or visit your doctor. Just count on Jesus.*" Or, "*You have lupus because you need to work on your bond with God.*" Whether it's mental or physical, a health problem is a health problem.

These messages confused me in my teens. I went to church, attended Catholic school from K–12th grade, served as a campus minister in high school and prayed daily. God was a huge part of my youth. So why was I struggling with depression if what the ministers said was true? I was bubbly in public, but at times secretly carried sadness. Being bullied in middle school hurt my self-esteem tremendously. I attended great schools, earned high grades and had a supportive family. I even had a telephone in my bedroom and a pager, which was a big deal for a teenager in the '90s. What was there to be sad about? So I prayed harder while feeling ashamed that I needed therapy. However, many Americans receive psychological treatment. The Substance Abuse and Mental Health Services Administration (SAMHSA) reports one-in-five adults live with a mental health challenge.

In college, I wrestled with my faith and depression. I felt God had abandoned me. Eventually, I met other wonderful people on campus who lived with depression and realized my condition wasn't a result of me not being Christian enough. I released my internal shame when I began working in mental health advocacy. One of my responsibilities included hosting a mental health podcast. Every day I interacted with people who were living active lives while managing bipolar disorder, depression, schizophrenia, PTSD, and so on. Their mental health conditions haven't gone away, but many said their spirituality helps them maintain their wellness. I heard this from Muslims, Christians, Buddhists, etc.

According to a 2010 survey by the California Mental Health and Spirituality Initiative, 79% of people with mental health challenges and family members agreed spirituality is important to their mental health. The percentage varies in different cultures. For example, 88% of African Americans agreed their faith is significant for their mental health.

"*Faith and spirituality are very important parts of culture,*" said Minister Monique Tarver, a mental health and spirituality expert. "*They provide hope and meaning to life, which are essential components to maintaining individual and community wellness.*"

One such example is Kompha Seth, co-founder of the Cambodian Association of Illinois. Seth lost his wife, child and most of his family during the Khmer Rouge genocide in Cambodia that lasted from 1975 to 1979. During an interview with him on the podcast, he told me that practicing Buddhism helps him and others in his community handle the effects of trauma.

"*Suffering is like fire,*" said Seth. "*The fire can burn the home or cook the food. In the philosophy of Buddhism, suffering is a part of us. How to be happy is to learn how to cope with it, live with it and overcome it.*"

Whether you believe in a higher power or not, anyone can have a mental health problem. Life happens. So does recovery. For years I falsely believed a weak bond with God led to my depression. Today, I see miracles through my work. I see the power of hope from people who have overcome unimaginable trials. I see the God in them. I see the God in me.

MIND CARE

Give love to my mind
Cradle my mind
Eat healthy for my mind
Get fresh air for my mind
Move my body for my mind
Sing to my mind
Be cautious of who and what I expose to my mind
Protect my mind
When crappy thoughts rise, change my mind
Say good things to my mind
Be gentle with my mind
Care for my mind

EVEN STRONG WOMEN GET DEPRESSED

MY EARLY BATTLES WITH depression began around 14 years old. The years of enduring bullying for being smart and having darker skin started to affect me. I fell into a deep, deep sadness. People told me to "cheer up," ignore the haters and be strong. I mentally beat myself up for not feeling strong enough. I was a talented, young Black woman from East Oakland with a bright future. However, I thought depression was hindering me from becoming the strong Black woman that is expected of women in my community.

When depression hit me hard my first year at UC San Diego, I still saw myself as weak. This made me feel less authentic as a Black woman. I was trying to recover from the madness of the O.J. Simpson Trial. It still was a hot topic a year-and-a-half after the verdict. The family issues I brushed under my mental rug weighed me down. Stress from my classes and the lack of diversity on campus didn't help either. I put myself down for feeling sadness when relatives or "friends" intentionally tried to hurt me. I didn't have the "forget you" attitude. I could not simply let it go. Depression takes more than just cheering up. I struggled to get out of that abyss for years.

We've equated being a strong woman to not breaking when life hurls its worst at you. This idea keeps some of us from getting counseling and feeling our feelings. Some of us suppress our pain with drugs, alcohol, food, bad relationships, etc. After college, I took a mindfulness class at Kaiser Hospital in Oakland. The instructor told us when we have a feeling, just feel it. It may be tough, but it will pass. However, she said the key is to be mindful of how we react to our feelings. For instance, if you're angry and hurt because of a failed relationship, let those feelings run through your body. Recognize those feelings, have compassion for yourself. Don't go out and do a Jazmine Sullivan on your heartbreaker's car.

Luckily I had great therapists who helped me. Through a lot of self-reflection, reading books by people like Iyanla Vanzant, watching Oprah's shows on spirituality, mindfulness, prayer, journaling and talking to others, I learned to have compassion for myself. Then I saw the strong woman in me.

I realized it takes a strong woman to ask for help. It takes a strong woman to feel her feelings, even when it hurts like hell. It takes a strong woman to accept she has a mental health challenge and to love herself. It takes a strong woman to excel while managing her depression. It takes a strong woman to take care of both her physical and mental health. Even when I'm not lifting myself up, it takes a strong woman to recognize that with compassion and try again.

Society has its expectations of what it means to be a strong woman, and in my case, a strong Black woman. Those expectations weren't good for my wellness. I hope if you are struggling with any mental health challenge, that you get help. Or even if your depression stems from a bad event in your life (i.e. a death, an injury, financial problems, torn relationship, violence), I hope you talk to someone. One in five Americans have a mental health challenge. You're not alone. Trust when I say there's probably someone in your life with a mental health problem. You may not even know it.

Getting help doesn't make you weak. It help makes you stronger.

REAP AND SOW

Instead of wishing for hail storms
To pound the lives
Of those
Who hurt you

Pray for blessings
To rain down
On you

For love to
Flow into your life

Pray for the healing of your heart

You'll enjoy those results
Much more

Trust me

LITTLE PIECE OF HEAVEN CHECKLIST

✓ Soak in a warm, candlelit, lavender bath. Play Kem or India.Arie to settle the mind. Stay in as long as you need.

✓ Dry off, then lather on your coconut-almond body butter. Rub it on lovingly.

✓ Give the girls a break. Leave your bra hanging on the doorknob.

✓ Slide on your favorite pair of cotton, parachute-style, granny panties. The ones with the faded pink and yellow daisies.

✓ Your phone rings. Go see who it is. Let it go to voicemail.

✓ Head to the kitchen. The cook (that's you) is off tonight. Open the container of left over shrimp pad thai. Reheat.

✓ Uncork the bottle of wine your friend bought you on your birthday trip to Napa. You'll probably smile about something funny from the trip as you pour.

✓ Sit on the couch in your granny panties with a glass of wine, chopsticks and shrimp pad thai.

✓ Bless your food.

✓ Make the hardest decision of the night. Watch Chris Rock standups on Netflix or your Love Jones DVD?

✓ Whatever you choose, watch until you're just about to fall asleep.

✓ Remind yourself to do this more often.

GEORGIA LOVER

He made me feel like
I was light as southern mist
And sweet as peach pie

ROOM 359

We made love
In Room 359

We made young, broke, 20-something, just out of college,
Dorito-dust fingers, empty Boone's bottles,
Long distance lovers
Getaway love

We did it like no one who stayed there before
Like no one was next door
Like the days had no hours

We sealed our sweaty brown bodies
Under stiff, chalky sheets
While tour pamphlets and condom wrappers
Lay across the floor

A refuge away from
Deadlines, expiration dates and
What's next after college?

Over four days we
Licked and kissed
In a timeless space
A mini paradise of laughter,
Our private poetry reading,
And cable TV

Where worries died before speaking them
Shhhh, don't even talk about it

On that final morning
We made love
Like we would never see each other again

Then time intruded
In the form of a wakeup call from the front desk
He had a flight to catch
I had to get on the road

We moved in silence
Broken by the rustle of me
Brushing my hands
In his hair

We dressed
Carried our luggage and memories
Leaving the room keys
Behind

PERFECT TIMING

It's funny how they say *perfect timing*
Because one's *perfect timing* is another's
Second too soon
Minute too late
Or
If only I had more time

Like how her perfect timing was my
I took too long
I wasn't ready
I need time to think
It might not be the right time for us

Tick, tock, tick, tock

But you came into her life at the perfect time
And by the time I was ready...
5, 4, 3, 2, 1, 0
It was
Too late

Time was on her side when she met you
The day after I left
27 hours after we fought to be exact
Which was about 42,600 minutes
Before your commitment to her

When I felt the time was
Right
Tick, tock, tick tock
Your love
Left

You said I took too much time
You couldn't wait
But I needed to take my time
Didn't we have all the time in the world?

My time is up?
For real?

Time waits for no one
You couldn't wait for me

We didn't finish the discussion because
It was almost time for you to meet her
You're never late

I can't go back in time and change this

Time, you weren't on my side

They say time heals a broken heart
I hope in my case
Time flies

LAUNDRY BLUES

Baby
I found some panties in the dryer
And I know they're not mine
I said I found some panties in the dryer
You know I don't wear
No size nine

Baby
Don't give me no
See, what happened was story
Because what you have to say won't be true
Said I don't want to hear no
See, what happened was story
Because I wouldn't B. S. with you

Baby
Ending this isn't easy
But I have to look out for me
No ending this isn't easy
But I don't want some STD

Now
Just leave the key on the table
Loving you hurts more than
Thorns on a rose

That's right
Leave the key on the table
Go find some other girl
To fold your damn clothes

MATURING INTO PRINCE

MY AUNT AND I were my family's version of Rudy and Vanessa from *The Cosby Show*. When I was six and she 16, we often got into arguments over one of the biggest issues of the 1980s.

"*Prince is BETTER!*" she'd yell.

"*No, he isn't! Michael Jackson is the best forever!*" I yelled back.

"*Prince is cooler and people like him more. He'll win more awards than Michael Jackson. PRINCE IS THE BEST!*"

"*YOU'RE MEAN!*" I screamed on the verge of tears.

"*Hey, cool it!*" my grandmother shouted from the kitchen. She didn't want us to wake up my grandfather who worked nights.

I was too young to get Prince at the time. *The Controversy* album poster, where he's in the shower with his chest hairs and speedo, hung in my aunt's closet. Sometimes I snuck in her room when her closet door was open to get a peek. Prince being wet and nearly naked, with a crucifix on the shower wall, perplexed my six-year-old mind. *Why is he posing all nasty with a cross in the shower? Does Grandma know this poster is in here?* Prince's Blackness and how he expressed gender as a Black man were foreign to me.

I was not only too young to understand Prince. I wasn't allowed to understand him. My Catholic grade school banned him. Teachers took away any Prince paraphernalia students wore or brought to school. Saying the name Prince cost you time on the bench during recess. I'm serious. I took one of my aunt's buttons to school just to see what would happen. A kid snitched on me. My teacher confiscated the button and added it to the pile of Prince merchandise in her drawer. I don't recall the school's reasoning for the Prince ban. I assume it had to do with his sexiness and pushing gender boundaries.

I finally grew into Prince in my early 20s. One of my Sigma sorority sisters in Los Angeles, who is a big fan, opened my heart to Prince. I sat in the car listening to an old school station. "When Doves Cry" came on. I heard the song before, but this time I really listened. That opening guitar riff seduced me. I was recovering from a bad break up at the time. Like the song, someone I cared about made me feel alone in a cold world. I loved the rawness and vulnerability in the lyrics. I felt his emotions when he alternated the pitch in his voice. The song spoke to my soul. I bought the *The Ultimate Prince Collection* CD from Circuit City that day and have been under his purple spell ever since.

I began to understand him: broadening ideas of Blackness and manhood, breaking gender norms, being unashamed about sexual desire, looking at the complexities of love, embracing being different, challenging an industry notorious for stealing from Black artists, and celebrating life. I get it now.

In 2009, Michael Jackson died. I was living in Los Angeles and drove to his star on the Hollywood Walk of Fame to pay my respects with the other fans. Many of us had a feeling Michael Jackson's days were numbered because of his behavior. M. J.'s passing hurt. Prince's death seven years later hit me harder because it was unexpected.

After his death, I celebrated him in a short purple dress, fishnets and boots at the Cat Club in San Francisco for a Prince-themed night. I regret never seeing Prince live in concert. I was living in Oakland when he gave one of his last performances. I needed to save money because I was unemployed. I decided to wait for him to return for a future show. Big mistake.

Who do I think is better between Prince and the King of Pop? Both artists were geniuses who left us too soon, ironically because of pharmaceutical drugs (our drug culture and Big Pharma taking advantage of people is another issue). I will neither compare the two, nor give my aunt the satisfaction of thinking she's been right all of these years. I still play their music. There's room in my heart for both of them and space on my closet wall for a Prince poster.

REST STOP

I'm running on four hours of sleep, a broken heart, and a stomachache

Over time I served him my affection
On fine china and white tablecloths
By candlelight

Yesterday he devoured my heart
Wiped the crumbs from his face
Smacked his lips
Licked his fingers
And picked the remains
Out of his teeth

A loud, long, gurgling belch rose deep
From his belly

He stretched his greasy hands to mine
Looked me in my eyes
Smiled
Then said, *Thanks for the meal babe, but it's over*
You don't excite me anymore

He untucked the soiled cloth napkin
From between his tuxedo shirt and chest hairs
Then dropped it on the dirty dish

He excused himself from the table
I always took care in preparing for him

I'm running on 4 hours of sleep, a broken heart, and a stomachache

He shuts the door
I close my heart and open the icebox

The merlot is chilled
Reaching for the bottle I see
Lemons picked from my grandparents' tree
Sixty-five years of lemons from that tree

I want the merlot
But I make lemonade
Re-learning how
To make the bitter into sweet

I'm running on 4 hours of sleep, a broken heart, and a stomachache

Mama says
Give him a chance
Maybe something is going on with him
Baby he got an Ivy League degree

I tell Mama I don't care if he graduated from Oxford

Mama is silent.
She apologizes with her silence
Then Mama says, *His loss!*
She gives me good advice
Don't let him rent space in your head

I'm running on 4 hours of sleep, a broken heart and a stomachache

The doctors say my grandmother is in early stages of dementia
But I don't want to believe it
I tell her all of the good men are taken
She says
Baby, men are everywhere. They walkin' down the street,
In the grocery store, at the gas station, the mall
I could get me a man right now if I wanted to

The disease tries to steal her mind, but it can't take her spice
I laugh, then tears stream down my face
My grandma's spice turns to sugar
She says,
Now you ain't need him, or the others before him, to come into this world
Ya hear?

Dementia can't steal her heart either

I'm running on 4 hours of sleep, a broken heart, and a stomachache

I get on Facebook to think about something else
What was I thinking?
I'm disturbed by the silence I hear and see

We cry justice for Black men and boys
Lynched by police

Our silence for Mitrice Richardson—INJUSTICE
Our silence for Dee Whigham—INJUSTICE
Our silence for Deborah Danner—INJUSTICE
Our silence for Black women and girls beaten, murdered and raped by
Police
Celebrities
Athletes
The neighbor
That weird uncle you know damn well
Shouldn't be invited to family functions

ALL INJUSTICES

My sistas it feels like it's just us
In this fight for our justice
And that's too painful to accept

We there for them
Not enough are there for us
Sistas, some of us
Aren't there for us

My God I'm sick and tired
Of being sick and tired!

I'm running on 4 hours of sleep, a broken heart, and a stomachache

This part of the journey
Is too rough
To go on

I need a rest stop
Is there a rest stop for love, for Black women?
Is there a rest stop for love, for me?

FAIRYTALES

He sings like a beauty
But is a beast at breaking hearts
He who shall not be named
A Pied Piper
I danced to his song
Too long

He's magnificent
At being maleficent
I thought I was woke
To dudes like him
Maybe I was in a deep sleep of denial

Or just hooked
On what I mistook
For love
That was really
Some mythical, screwy
Wonderland where I fell
Down a deep hole
Landing in Never
I pray I never, ever, never, ever
Meet a man who melts my heart
Then turns me into an
Ice queen

Poor me
He has no soul
I won't stay silent
About how he did me wrong

So many nights the clock strikes twelve
He's still on my mind,
My heart

I want to get rid of him
Wish him away

I just haven't figured out
How to make him say
His name backwards

ELOHSSA
ELOHSSA
ELOHSSA

BURGER

My relationships are like sliders
They're nibbles of what I desire
Like love, trust and intimacy
Like watching movies at home on rainy nights and
Eating stove-popped popcorn
Like being embraced in warm arms
While my head rides
On the calm rise and fall of his chest

Those nibbles taste good
But I'm never satisfied
My plate gets empty quickly
Before I can savor anything
They leave
Never staying around for the entree

I'm tired of ordering love
From the appetizer menu

I want the full burger
The Works
I want juicy, quarter pounder, organic, double patty,
High calorie love

Love so big
You can barely hold it in your hands
You can't finish in two bites

Love so big
You have to take your time to
Work through it

Chew slowly, don't chomp
Eat it mindfully

Take in the seasonings, the salt, the oil, the pickles, the veggies, the relish
Realize the little things that make the burger
Mean a lot

Hold the secret sauce
Be real with me and
Honest about all of the ingredients
That make up who you are
Be true to me

And NO side orders
No onion rings
No regular fries, garlic fries, sweet potato fries,
Criss-cut fries, seasoned fries
No side chick-en fingers
Nothing on the side
No one on the side
Just the burger
Just the main dish
Just us

But you can sip on my chocolate shake
And taste my apple pie

I want bacon on my burger
Why?
Because everything is better with bacon!

I want the entire burger
I want it so good that the
Mustard and ketchup drip
Out of the corners of your mouth
And stain your shirt

The burger gets messy
But you're committed
We'll try to get the stains out
We'll work hard to get the stains out

Even if they don't come all the way out
You know it was worth the burger
You know it was worth every bite
You know I'm worth it
We're worth it

I want the whole damn burger
Even the onions that stink up your breath
Even the mushroom and lettuce wedged in your teeth
Even the gas and indigestion
Like relationships,
Eating burgers ain't pretty all the time

But we'll take Tums and toothpicks
And eat again
And love again

I want the entire burger
The special burger
That fills our stomachs, hearts and souls

I want that burger that we'll always remember
As the best we've ever had

We won't order to go
This is no fast food burger
No drive thru burger

We'll sit down

Dinner is for here
At this table
For two
For now
Forever

Bon Appétit
Love is now served

THE DANCE

Out of all the women
He asked her to dance
A tall Black vessel
Home to a beautiful soul
As handsome as he was on the outside

His hands equally strong as gentle
Reached out to her
She said yes
With glimmering brown eyes

He led her to the dance floor
Then to his heart
She sank into his body
Transferring all of the pain
To his touch
Healing
Finally someone gave her the gift
To be vulnerable

His embrace melted away the callous
On her spirit
Left by life's hardships
Finally someone let her be soft
Be free

She felt his longing to be loved
To be seen
Gently
Finally somebody knew
He mattered

While everyone else twerked it, worked it, shook it up,
Turnt it out

They swayed
Twirled
To their own song
No one else existed
They formed their own world
In this rhythmic embrace
Living to their own beat

When the DJ said last call
They locked eyes
Smiles curled up their lips
It may have been the last call
But it wasn't their
Last dance

IN YOUR BODY

Relax your mind
Close your eyes
Breathe in
Breathe out
Ahhhhhhhh
Breathe in
Breathe out
Ahhhhhhhhh
Be in your body
Yes, be in your body
Every part of your body
Feel the sensations
The urges
The desires
Feel the intensity
Let that energy run
Flow
In your body
Your wonderful, miraculous vessel
Breathe in
Breathe out
Open your eyes
Look across at your lover
Enter the windows of each other's souls
Embrace, hearts touching
Hold
Be in this moment
Caress slowly
Caress
Be in your body
Enjoy its response to touch
Delight in the tickles of your lover's finger tips
Against your lips
Your neck

Your shoulders
Your breasts
Respond
Caress them slowly
Caress
Do you notice their body's response to your touch?
Amazing
Take a breath
Ahhhhh
Your body is warming
Beautiful
Deep breath
Hmmmmmm
Groan
Moan
Giggle
As loud as you want
Let your skin and spirit drink in
Every drop of
Pleasure
Be in your body and
Your spirit

WHEN THE PETALS DRY

She thought she was invincible
The world was just a pebble in her hand
Nothing to fear
Nothing could overwhelm her

She was the girl who birthed dreams in the front seat of her mamma's car
Wanted a life beyond cracked sidewalks littered with
Bullet shells and pain
She was the girl who knew that her worth
Lived infinitely between her ears
And in her spirit

Life's rain was a puddle she skipped over
God was deep rooted in the core of her soul

Then she grew older
The world she thought she knew
Tumored into a boulder too heavy for her scarred hands

Her heart became infertile to dreams
The same cracks she longed to escape
Mirrored her fears

She reduced her worth to their opinions
Valued herself as less than what they
Abandoned her for

Years passed
She grew
Found wisdom in her tribulations
Recognized her strengths
Used faith to crush boulders into gravel

She listened to the inner child

Who said she could do anything
Silenced the hinderers
Used her own voice

She keeps growing
With the
Courage to
Love
Herself

LOVE MY PAIN AWAY

ONE OF MY FAVORITE posts on the mental health blog *Mad In America*[1] is by psychotherapist Dr. Michael Cornwall. He wrote about the healing power of love when we're in an emotional crisis, and how our culture's idea of competition and individualism causes us to suffer. I would add individualism makes some of us ashamed to ask for help.

Dr. Cornwall wrote, "*Fear, shame, guilt, despair and anger take up so much of the emotional space in the collective and solitary rooms we live in. Those painful emotions are the emotional currency of a culture that long ago lost its way from the ideals of altruism and justice.*"

He later shared stories of helping psychiatric patients, who were mute, open up by showing love and compassion for their suffering. Sometimes the therapy we need is love and affection.

In the midst of dealing with a number of deaths and praying my toxic job wouldn't kill me, I realized counseling wasn't enough. I had a great therapist. She gave me the right tools and support, but I got to a point where I needed someone to hold me. If you grew up in a loving household as a kid, adults were always giving you hugs or consoling you when you fell. Where do you go when you're a single, grown woman with bills and responsibilities? Where do you go when the people who would console you are part of the reason why you need love and affection? Or the people you usually turn to are going through their own problems? I was embarrassed to ask for a healing embrace. When friends greeted me with a hug, I absorbed as much as I could.

During a training at my former job, we split into groups and practiced peer-counseling tactics through role plays. My group gathered in the office's cramped, windowless kitchen. It's funny how God works because two people performed a scenario that mirrored what I was going through. One person needed counseling because she was taking care of her dying grandfather. The other played a friend who acted like a jerk while she was suffering through the loss. It was like watching myself. I felt the kitchen shrinking. My body temperature rose from struggling not to cry. The people who made up the scenario had no idea of what I was dealing with in my personal life. This must have been divine intervention. I jetted out of the kitchen to my office and cried. My younger co-worker came to my office and gave me the hug that I was dying for. She has a good heart because this wasn't a cry with a few teardrops. It was a sobbing, snotty, ugly cry with lots of venting. My co-worker kept encouraging me to let it out. I will forever be grateful to her for consoling me.

My co-worker's healing touch and compassion was the emotional remedy I needed. We rock and hold our babies, but we still need to do that for each other in adulthood. Even embracing a pet helps. There are so many people fronting like everything is fine and under control. In reality they are filled pain. I usually post a reminder to my CocoaFly.com followers to check in with people; even the ones you think have it easy. Most of us are dealing with some kind of challenge in life. During the ups and downs, we need love on the regular.

Going back to Dr. Cornwall's post, I think some of us don't ask for affection because we fear being seen as pathetic or needy. In the hook to Rihanna's "Love Song" featuring Future, he questions if asking for love and affection makes him come off desperate. Babies can die from not being held enough and loved. Honestly, I believe some adults do, too. We turn to unhealthy habits to make us feel good. Needing love and affection is nothing to be ashamed of. It's natural.

According to an article from *Psychology Today*,[2] there are health benefits to hugging. Consensual embraces reduce levels of the stress hormone cortisol. Contact can lower your blood pressure and heart rate. Hugging also releases the love hormone oxytocin, which increases feelings of connection.

I know there are people I could've called and said, *"Hey, I need a hug."* My pride stopped me. If one of my friends called me and said they needed a hug, I would be right there, without judgment. So I shouldn't judge myself. I'm human. Lesson learned. Thankfully, those hardships that caused my ugly cry have passed. Asking for a hug still isn't always easy for me, but I can't afford to let my pride get in the way of my self-care.

1. Cornwall, Michael. "The Elusive Emotional Wound Our Culture Inflicts on Us and the Healing Balm of Love that Can Heal Them." Mad In America. 2016 May 15. www.madinamerica.com.

2. Polard, Andrea F. "4 Benefits of Hugs, for Mind and Body." Psychology Today. 08 June 2014. www.psychologytoday.com.

THE PURPLE ROSE WHO BLOOMS

I am the purple rose who blooms
Sprouting
In a concrete jungle
Reaching for the sun's glory

I am the purple rose who blooms
Petals colored with
Blood and ink
Sapphire and rubies
Fire and ocean
Good lovin' and the blues

I am the purple rose who blooms
At times I've grown during long droughts
Alone in the darkness
Reminding myself
I am my own star

My stem rooted
Never snapping
I bend with the wind gusts
Stand in the storm
Even when it hurts
But somehow come out brighter
Glowing right with the rainbows

I am the purple rose who blooms
I flourish most when I'm respected, protected,
Tended to, not neglected
I flourish when love shines on me

I am the purple rose who blooms
There is no figure to match my worth
I'm not here for anyone's picking

I am the purple rose who blooms
Vibrantly
For the little Black girls who are lied to
Told their dreams are impossible
I reflect possibility

I am the purple rose who blooms
I'm not a miracle
But the result of what my ancestors sowed
My greatness is natural

I am the purple rose who blooms

ACKNOWLEDGEMENTS

I've wanted to write a book since I learned how to hold a pen. I didn't get to this point alone. I give God the praise for this blessing and for bringing special people into my life who helped me become an author.

Mom, remember our trips to the library and Waldenbooks? You introduced me to literature. There are not enough words to express my gratitude for your love and encouragement. You always believe in me, even when I want to give up. I'm blessed to have you, my love at first heartbeat. And you're right, it all started with that little brown journal.

Thank you to my grandparents: the Kesees, Dardens, and Carraways. I treasure the culture and wisdom you passed on to me. You spoke greatness into me when I was a child and I stand on your shoulders. For those of you who are ancestors now, thank you for still watching over me.

To my father, from your example I learned the power of Philippians 4:13. The first book I ever appeared in was your memoir. You and Mom instilled in me the importance of learning about Black artists and writers. I'm grateful for that exposure because it allowed me to see I could be a writer too. I still use the Eso Won Bookstore tote bag you gave me when I was a teenager. Now I can carry my own book in it.

A heartfelt thank you to J. K. Fowler and the Nomadic Press family for believing in my work. Thank you for giving a voice to writers from marginalized communities and allowing us to be authentic. What you do is so important and I appreciate you.

I'm lucky to be edited by MK Chavez, one of my favorite writers on the planet. MK, working with you on my very first book was a dream come true. Thank you for your knowledge and support on this project.

Much love to my true friends. You are there for me during hardships and when it's time to get our party on. You always have my back and I'm forever grateful. I love ya'll!

Sisterly love to my sophisticated, genuine and radiant sorors of Sigma Gamma Rho. Thank you sorors for your support over the years. I'm so glad God led me to the RHOyal Blue and Gold path.

For every relative, teacher, mentor, and community member who told me to "keep going," I thank you. Thank you to all of the writing communities and curators who welcome me to their events. I appreciate that you open up spaces for writers to express themselves, especially during these times.

I have to give a special shout out to all of my CocoaFly.com followers! Thank you for engaging with me online and supporting my work since 2008. Many of you have said my work inspires you, but I've gained so much learning from you, too.

For anyone I overlooked, please charge it to my head and not my heart.

Previous publications include:

Los Angeles Times (March 10, 2016): "Growing Up Darden and Dealing with the Racial Backlash from the O. J. Simpson Trial"

Huffington Post: "I'm Depressed Because I Don't Have a Good Relationship with God?"

Cocoafly.com: "Even Strong Women Get Depressed," "Love My Pain Away"

JENEÉ DARDEN is an award-winning journalist, public speaker, mental health advocate, and proud Oakland native. She has reported for NPR, *Time Magazine*, *The LA Times*, *Ebony*, *Refinery 29*, *The Establishment*, KQED and other outlets. Jeneé covers issues related to women, race and wellness on her website and podcast CocoaFly.com. During her down time, this former National Book Foundation summer fellow enjoys dancing and watching superhero movies. The daughter of O. J. Simpson Trial prosecutor Christopher Darden, Jeneé holds a BA in ethnic studies from UC San Diego and a master's degree in journalism from the University of Southern California.